Yorkshire & Lincolnshire Verses

Edited by Michelle Afford

YoungWriters
First published in Great Britain in 2007 by:
Young Writers
Remus House
Coltsfoot Drive
Peterborough
PE2 9JX
Telephone: 01733 890066
Website: www.youngwriters.co.uk

SB ISBN 1 84602 738 1

Foreword

Young Writers was established in 1991 and has been passionately devoted to the promotion of reading and writing in children and young adults ever since. The quest continues today. Young Writers remains as committed to the nurturing of poetic and literary talent as ever.

This year's Young Writers competition has proven as vibrant and dynamic as ever and we are delighted to present a showcase of the best poetry from across the UK and in some cases overseas. Each poem has been selected from a wealth of *A Pocketful Of Rhyme* entries before ultimately being published in this, our fourteenth primary school poetry series.

Once again, we have been supremely impressed by the overall quality of the entries we have received. The imagination, energy and creativity which has gone into each young writer's entry made choosing the poems a challenging and often difficult but ultimately hugely rewarding task - the general high standard of the work submitted ensured this opportunity to bring their poetry to a larger appreciative audience.

We sincerely hope you are pleased with this final collection and that you will enjoy *A Pocketful Of Rhyme Yorkshire & Lincolnshire Verses* for many years to come.

Contents

The Poems

Autumn Leaves

Dead leaves
Giant legs
Bumpy bark
Golden leaves
Chocolate trunks
Feel the winter breeze
Ruby-red leaves
Leaves swaying in the breeze
The birds singing to me
Branches battle
Feel the breeze
Conkers lying.

Amelia O'Neill (7)
Anlaby Junior School, Anlaby

Trees Are Reeds

Trees
The rustling reeds
Rustling in
The breeze
Turning, tossing in the
Breath of someone
Blowing gently
Come the squawking crows
Landing silently.
Then come summer flowers
Blooming steadily in winter.
Come snowy snow, gently
Flowing through the air
Looking for a place to land
Time to go away
I'm like a bit of bone that is
From a giant's leg
But broken in half.
It's cranky and old
Like a wrinkly
Grandma or grandad.

Melissa Hamilton (7)
Anlaby Junior School, Anlaby

Trees

Branches blowing in the wind.
Leaves whispering.
Trees rustling in the sky.
The leaves swaying in the sky.
Blustering branches bowing.
Birds tweeting in the sky.
Wavy brown tree.
Like a castle in the sky.
Like giant's fingers.
Chocolate fingers.
The singing birds sing to me
Leaves fall off the trees.
Bark on the ground with trees.
Branch breaking, ruby-red leaves.
Gold birds and blossom candyfloss.
Crushed, baited leaves.
Trees in the breeze.

Charlie Doonan (7)
Anlaby Junior School, Anlaby

Trees

Trees bowing to me.
Leaves falling.
Birds singing for me.
Leaves crunching.
Leaves munching.
You can smell the trees' leaves.
You can see the branches breaking.
You can taste the chocolate bark.
Break it off.
You can see the ruby-red leaves.
You can see the fiery red leaves.
You can feel the air
Blowing through my hair.
You can see babies in prams.
You can hear babies crying.
You can see cars passing.

Jamie Lees (7)
Anlaby Junior School, Anlaby

Trees

Branches blowing in the breeze
Glowing leaves in the trees
Giant leaves blowing in the wind
Busy bees on the leaves
Ruby-red leaves like red traffic lights
Crunchy leaves like crisps
Thick branches like fat pens
The bark is damp like a muddy football shirt
Wind whispering in the air
It's a misty morning
Dinner's cooking
Trees are looking.

Emma-Jayne Johnson (7)
Anlaby Junior School, Anlaby

Trees

Trees are breaking.
The trees stop making . . .
Old like old men.
They are like devils' beanstalks.
They look very mean.
No colour on the trees.
They have brown knobbly bumps.
The trees look very cold.
Leaves swaying.
Wind swaying through the trees.
Spring is coming.

Lewis Massey (7)
Anlaby Junior School, Anlaby

The Snow

I am the snow
I dance from the sky
I tiptoe from the sky to the earth.

When I get down to earth I cover the grass
I hang from the trees
Sometimes I like to go to sleep in the trees.

I have a little nap in the snow
I like to hug the rest of the snow
And I cover the earth.

The sun comes out to shine
The sun smiles at me
I cry out loud
And now I am water.

Megan Bone (11)
Anlaby Junior School, Anlaby

Snow

I am the snow.
I'm dancing across the sky slowly and gracefully.
I cover the ground with my blanket.
I'm walking across the leaves.
I grip the tree with my icy fingers.
I cover the houses like a new can of paint.
I steal the summer and the happiness.
I bite the children's fingers.
I see the sun come out.
I retreat to the hills.
I watch.

Daniel Clark (10)
Anlaby Junior School, Anlaby

The Snow

I am snow.
I parachute from the clouds above, falling gracefully.
I have cold skin.
I dance, falling from the sky.

I wrap my arms around the land.
I sit on fields all alone.
I tickle the noses of children.
I start to fly like a bullet.

I start to cry.
The sun gets in my path.
I am trembling.
My body melts.

Kieran Liddell (11)
Anlaby Junior School, Anlaby

The Storm

I am a storm
Turning the outdoor lights on and off.
My fingers will prod your houses
I am nature's lumberjack.

I am a storm.
My winds sing beautiful songs.
I make cars go out of control
Moving clouds along for my next victim.

I am a storm
Drumming on the cars.
Clouds are crying
Knocking on your door.

I am a storm
Banging and booming.
Giving you a headache
Scaring children stiff.

I am a storm
Granting peace.
Waiting till it's time to strike
I am gone.

Oliver Cawkwell (10)
Anlaby Junior School, Anlaby

Snow Is Falling

I am the snow.
I parachute from the sky
Falling delicately and gracefully.
I cover the earth with a blanket
And wrap my cold arms around the city.

I cling like a bat to everything I pass.
I bite the noses of children as I come around.

I come to an end, my tears cry
Drip-drop,
Drip-drop.

Rebecca Gill (10)
Anlaby Junior School, Anlaby

The Snow

I am snow.
I parachute from the sky.
I hug and grip the ground.
The sky cries every night.
I rest on the ground.
I sleep on the ground.
I cover it like a white blanket.
I retreat to the mountains.
The sun smiles at me.
I lay there still.

Robyn Purdy (10)
Anlaby Junior School, Anlaby

The Snow Story

I am snow.
I parachute out of the sky
Falling delicately to the floor.
I cover the earth like a soft, white, cuddly blanket.

I am snow.
I lay on the floor in silence.
I cover sticks in white softness.
I hug the grass as if it's my teddy bear.

I am snow.
I lay with tears drifting down my face,
Drip-drop, drip-drop, drip.
Goodbye for another year.

Jed Pearson
Anlaby Junior School, Anlaby

The Big Bad Storm

I am a storm.
I spread dark clouds and my cloak of fear over the earth.
I destroy everything in my path.
I howl around the houses.
I always bring destruction.
I sometimes play tug of war with the trees and I always win.
I feel powerful as I shout my anger over the universe.
I am your worst nightmare as my tears fall over you.

Joseph Last & Bobbie Branton (11)
Anlaby Junior School, Anlaby

The Storm

I am a storm.
My angry fingers prod the earth.
I am nature's lumberjack
Destroying everything beneath me.
I'm nature's vandalising terror
Deluging the place beneath me
Playing a threatening tune.
I am nature's nightmare
I chop down trees at will.
Finally, my work is over
All I can do now is stay still.

Katie Melissa Rust (11)
Anlaby Junior School, Anlaby

Frostbite

Winter creeps across the land ready to attack
Darkness helping the wind along
While snow stays hovering at the back
Ice smirking, it knows it all
Frost happy, he's having a ball.

Cold breeze knocks at people's knees
The wind howling at the trees
Leaving them bare, shivering with fright
A lonely, dark, cold night.

Winter creeps across the land ready to attack
Darkness helping the wind along
While snow stays hovering at the back.
Ice smirking, it knows it all
Frost happy, he's having a ball.

Darkness smiles, it's conquered all
Snow gently starts to fall
Wrapping his frosty arms around Earth
Icicles shaking, ready to give birth.

Winter creeps across the land ready to attack
Darkness helping the wind along
While snow stays hovering at the back
Ice smirking, it knows it all
Frost happy, he's having a ball.

Trees drip from ice and snow
The darkness clearing, all is go
A bright light shines, all is gone
No more winter till next year.

Hannah Murray (10)
Anlaby Junior School, Anlaby

The Storm

I am a storm!
Booming and banging
Bringing darkness to the town
My angry fingers prodding the earth
Trees going up in bright orange flame
My wind screaming round your head like a banshee.

I give you a headache and bang on your car
Scaring little children stiff as concrete
I take aim and fire, disconnecting all your wires
You sit in darkness
I shout with glee.

Just then the rain stops
The clouds float away
The lightning starts to slow
And the thunder stops.
I am gone.

Joshua Sanders (10)
Anlaby Junior School, Anlaby

Storm

I am a storm!
Disconnecting all your wires
My angry fingers prod the earth
Bringing darkness to the town.
I'm nature's lumberjack
Destroying the trees
I'm one of nature's mysteries.
My angry stomps echo off buildings
Singing songs of sadness
Wailing with tears streaming from my eyes up in the skies
I tear the earth apart.
I drum on vehicles.
I knock on doors.
I tap on windows
And flood the floor.
Then shout, 'Hey you, I'm in charge!'

Bethany Watson (11)
Anlaby Junior School, Anlaby

I Am The Storm

I am the storm.
I bellow angrily as I wake everyone up from their peaceful sleep.
I bang my kettle drums causing echoes of deafness around the city.
My eerie black clouds declare war over the earth.
I crash down on the poor defenceless village frightening the children.
I demolish everything in my path.
Then I fly away to my sky-high home.
They think I'm gone forever but return I will.

Nathan Stowe (10)
Anlaby Junior School, Anlaby

Thunderstorms

I am the storm.
My endless, tawny fingers reach out to grab the emerald tree.
I roar at little children and screech at full-grown.
I dream when it's sun.
I boom when it's moon.
I am the shocking storm.
I am the dream breaker.
I bang my pots and pans when I'm angry.
I sob slightly and then pour out my cold tears.
I hate the heat of the sun, it blocks me out.

When moon comes and sun goes,
I dance around on beams of fire celebrating with strikes of light.
As I pass town by town, village by village,
I think of how proud Mother Storm would be of me.

Courtney Inch (10)
Anlaby Junior School, Anlaby

For I Am The Storm!

I am the storm.
I flash my blinding headlights across the midnight sky.
My sound scatters like confetti at a wedding, across the lonely town.
I scare the little children with my vicious roar.
I whimper and sob silently into starless heavens.
Then cackle, as my spell breaks and dies away.

Scarlett Alexander (10)
Anlaby Junior School, Anlaby

For I Am The Grass

I am the grass.
As an insect adventures up my endless stem I stand to attention.
The wind blows and I dance to its beat.
I tickle the children's feet as they run, laughing, to the pool.
Field mice and beetles hide in my garden.
I wave to passers-by and bow to the summer sun.
I long to reach the fiery stars.
I dream of being forever green.
I am soft and smooth, for I am the grass, tall or small.

Aimee Archibald (10)
Anlaby Junior School, Anlaby

What Am I?

I fall from the white fluffy clouds.
I tumble onto the stiff brown buildings.
I kiss the windowpane.
I dance upon the chimney pots.

Jodie Morgan (10)
Anlaby Junior School, Anlaby

Grass

I saw you dance along the floor below
And grow and grow and grow and grow.
Until, at last, you reached the sky
And then, eventually, I saw you die.

Ben Parish (10)
Anlaby Junior School, Anlaby

What Am I?

I shout and moan with anger,
I blow the houses away.
I strike the earth with my electric hands
As the people below run and hide.

I am the ruler of the sky
I whistle loud and high.
I get so sad, I start to cry.
The creatures below fear me.
I strike anything in my path.

What am I?

Thomas Dunn (10)
Anlaby Junior School, Anlaby

What Am I?

I moan and groan like a kid with no toy.
I strike and shout at the people below.
My belly rumbles with almighty thunder.
My wind howls like a hungry wolf.
My mean breeze freezes anybody who's in my way.
My thunder is a giant drum kit.
I jump miles in one footstep.

What am I?

Alex Withers (10)
Anlaby Junior School, Anlaby

Springing Spring

Hooray, spring has woken up
From a long winter's dream.

The sunflowers and tulips
Are dancing in pairs,
Kissing the green grass.
The roses and bluebells
Celebrate by singing happily.
The sun getting hotter now as they turn on the fire.

Girls giggling with the fairies
Making daisy chains on a blanket
Of soft, tickling, emerald-green grass.

Winter clothes are being chucked away
Bright green and yellow clothes
Are being taken out of the closet
While the schoolgirls put on their dresses.

The sun has got hotter now
And summer has come
Now it's time to say goodbye
As the flowers start to die away in the sun.

The fairies and flowers pack away their spring clothes
Because it's time to take out the swimming costumes for the summer holiday.

So now it's time to say goodbye
As the sun smiles its everlasting grin.

Haleema Parker (10)
Anlaby Junior School, Anlaby

Trees

Weeping branches swing.
Blossom is falling and swaying in the breeze.
Glittering leaves look bright on the trees.
Sparkling berries shine in the sun.
Crispy leaves on the ground.
Crushed sticks on the floor.
Dark, glittering branches come from their body.
The wind blows shuffling the branches,
Shooting conkers from the tree.
All is silent.

Ryan Cowling (7)
Anlaby Junior School, Anlaby

Trees

Golden leaves sparkling in the shimmering sun.
The leaves feel like old people's wrinkly hands.
The branches are dancing like a horse prancing.
The light leaves are like mucky feet.
I can hear the leaf's soft voice in the wind.
The trees are as high as the Eiffel Tower of Paris.
The trunk is a giant's foot.
In the gale, the leaves say my name,
The trees have got arms.

Amy Fenton (7)
Anlaby Junior School, Anlaby

Trees

Weeping branches
Leaping leaves
Melting ice cream
Crispy leaves
Towering trees
Enormous leaves
Choppy branches
Dancing leaves
Scattering branches
Swaying arms
Sleeping branches
Enormous slingers
Singing trees
Floor lickers
Rusty leaves
Conker branches
Snowy branches
Conker throwers
Powerful holders
Gentle swayers
Leaves swingers.

Maisie Drewry (7)
Anlaby Junior School, Anlaby

Trees

Hanging leaves sticking out from the branches.
Leaning trees tip to one side.
Long branches hold the leaves.
Giant tree trunks look like they touch the sky.
Falling leaves fall down as fast as they go.
Fat tree trunks stick out.
Skinny tree trunks squash together.
Cracking branches lean to one side.
Dull leaves lay on the ground.
Tall trees come up.
The trees have webs in them.
Leaves hang from long branches.
There are baby branches.
Weeds flop down.
The tree trunks feel bumpy.
They stick out.
Baby sticks fall onto the ground.
Some trees are so giant that they are as fat as the tree trunks.
Branches curl round as they stick out.
A few trees get chopped down from the old days.
As the wind blows, it is like the trees are talking to you.
It looks like the trees are dead when the wind has stopped.
The trees keep you out of the sun.
They put a shadow down.
Clever people can climb them.
I love trees.

Spencer Pearson (7)
Anlaby Junior School, Anlaby

Trees

Lovely leaping leaves love to dance like a ballerina.
Swaying branches rattle in the cool wind.
The conkers drop lightly like a feather.
The crunchy, crackly leaves crunch under your feet.
The top of the tree looks like ice cream melting.
You can smell the sweet scents of the crackling leaves.
The giant branches look like they are reaching out to get you
And the enormous trees look like they are towering over you.
The leaping leaves love to spring in the moonlight.
The branches of the trees look like a person reaching out to get a
sharp pointy pencil.
The gentle wind blows the sweet smell of bark; it crackles in your
hands like melted chocolate.
The leaves look like a balloon falling from the gigantic tree.
When the wind blows it looks like it is going to fall with a big *bang!*
If you look very carefully you will see some bark spreading out as
slow as a tortoise.
But when you see a branch move it looks like it really wants to
grab you.

Jane Grantham (7)
Anlaby Junior School, Anlaby

Trees

The weeping branches
Carefully rattle in
The breeze.
The lovely spring
Blossom trees,
When pretty
Blossom floats down
Onto the ground.
When the wind blows
And all the fresh air
Comes to me.
It gives me great
Pleasure to be
Outside.
The trees look like
They have hands with arms.
I can smell
The breeze in the air.
I can see children
Playing in the crispy leaves.
The really lovely
Leaves with bright
Colours are floating
In the air like tiny boats.
I can feel the breeze
In the air.
Trees are
Good for us.
They help us breathe.

Laura Wright (7)
Anlaby Junior School, Anlaby

Trees

The blossom trees were covered in tasty icing.
The blossom trees were dripping in sparkling white snow.
The wind was crashing against the tree trunks.
The wind was blowing on the rattling leaves.
The bumpy tree trunks were a funny shape.
The fat stalks on the trees were deep.
The delicious smells coming from the tasty berries.
The berries were very little.
The enormous trees were baggy and heavy.
The tree was very still, like it was staring at me.

Laura Withers (7)
Anlaby Junior School, Anlaby

Trees

Branches wibble and wobble.
Branches break.
They look like huge chocolate bars.
The leaves crunch like cornflakes.
The leaves shiffle and shuffle,
Raindrops splashing and splishing.
Raindrops falling on the grass like the grass has washed its hair.

Cameron Alexander (7)
Anlaby Junior School, Anlaby

Trees

I can see trees looking like their arms are spreading
So their wrinkly fingers can touch the sky.
I can hear gloomy leaves rustling like an old car running out of petrol.
I can see trees looking like they are ice cream melting in the bright
hot sun.
I can hear crispy leaves crunch and crackle under our feet.
The leaping leaves spring in the bright sun.
Leaves on top of the treetops look like somebody's hair being blown
by a hairdryer.
While the trees are not being blown by the wind it looks like they
are dead.
When the sides of the trees blow it looks like they are spreading out
a pair of wings.
The tree is as bumpy as a road.
The tree is as big as a giant.

Ehren Lewis (8)
Anlaby Junior School, Anlaby

Trees

Trees look like they are ice creams melting in the hot sun.
The chocolate tree trunk looks like it's delicious.
Crispy leaves crunch and crackle under your feet.
Weeping branches rattling in the gentle wind.
Colossal tree trunks surrounded by bark.
The trees looking like arms sticking out to touch the ground.
The branches look like arms and wrinkly fingers.
I can smell the gentle breeze flowing around the trees.
I can smell the great breeze in the air.
The trees look like they are talking.
The trees are growing slowly.
The trees look like they are dead.
The trees are large and small sizes.
The trees are jumbo fish fingers.

Daniel Cole (7)
Anlaby Junior School, Anlaby

What Are Trees Like?

Yellow sunny leaves,
Ruby-red on the trees.
Crunchy crisps,
Scattered everywhere,
Over there and over there
And soggy blankets
Covering the bark.
I can hear birds singing their tunes,
Leaves falling
To the ground
And the whistling sound they make.
The tunes they create
When the leaves
Come falling down.
Boys playing sword,
Fighting in the playground,
But then,
There goes the bell.
It is very quiet but
You know the trees
Are still playing
When you're not about.

Rowan Bye (7)
Anlaby Junior School, Anlaby

Trees

Trees
Blowing in the breeze
Yellow sunny leaves
Ruby-red on the trees
Leaves crunching
Like crisps munching
Giant broccoli
Towering over me
The bark is rough
And it smells like broth.

Daniel Murray (8)
Anlaby Junior School, Anlaby

Trees

The leaves rustling in the breeze
Trunks with knobbly knees
Bark like metal
Ruby-red leaves
Glowing golden
Singing sparrows
Crowing crows
Wild wind
Green grass
Skiddy grass
Rough bark
Devil stork
Wrinkled broccoli
Witch's fingers
Robins repeating
Boiling beans
Trees lean
Dinner cooking
Trees looking.

Connor Bibby (7)
Anlaby Junior School, Anlaby

Trees

Trunks with knobbly knees
Smell honey from the bees.

Leaves munching
Like crisps crunching.

The owls hide out to
The hunters wipe out.

Leaves
Like green, green grass
With a trunk
Like chocolate fingers.

Blossom like fluffy candyfloss
Beavers listen to their boss.

Wind with waves
Trees are saved.

Joseph Bastable (7)
Anlaby Junior School, Anlaby

Trees

Whistling wind
Like a teddy in the sky.
It's a castle in the sky,
Branch breaking like a fly.
The bark is rough
And the sky is high.
The clouds are fluffy
Nice and puffy.
The mud is like melted chocolate.
Swirling wind, all is quiet.

Georgina Cross (7)
Anlaby Junior School, Anlaby

Trees

Trees, trees.
Wind whisper
In the leaves.
Trees, trees.
God's breath
In the trees.
Trees, trees.
The tree,
Look bark,
Growing out
Of the ground.
Trees, trees.
Taste the
Bark and air to
Make strong
Breath blow
Into leaves.
Trees, trees.
Bumpy bark,
Conkers free.

Eve Barker (7)
Anlaby Junior School, Anlaby

My Family

I live at home with my mum, dad and Finlay
We have lots of pets, too many to mention
They need lots of love, time and attention.

There's Zeus the buzzard
Patrick the rabbit
Laddie the dog
Aslan and Lucy, the golden lizards
And let's not forget
Last but not least
Lots of fish that look nice enough to eat.

My daddy feeds Zeus, her baby chicks
Aslan and Lucy, live crickets they eat, *yuck!*
Patrick the rabbit eats anything that's crunchy
Laddie eats anything, especially when he's hungry.
The fish eat food especially prepared by Daddy
We have to keep them away from Laddie.

When I am at home
I am most happy
Especially when I am with Finlay, Mummy and Daddy.

Phoebe Scott (7)
Blackburn Primary School, Rotherham

The Seaside

The swerving, curving
Sea crashes against the rocks.
The waves are very high.
They nearly touch the sky.

When the swerving, curving
Sea crashes against the rocks,
I think to myself, *I've seen the cops.*

Kayleigh Unwin (7)
Blackburn Primary School, Rotherham

A Hamster's Life

In the shop I run around,
Trying to be the first to be picked from the ground.
When I'm picked I scramble much,
Waiting to be moved to my new hutch.

In my hutch there's a Ricky G,
But he is not near to me.
I also have a large wheel,
And it is near to my meal.

On the second day I'm in my ball
Bumping into the solid wall.
Then I'm handled for a little while
And then they stop me from running a mile.

During the day I like to sleep
I like to burrow nice and deep.
In the night I like to play,
When all the people have gone away.

Yvonne Billard (8)
Blackburn Primary School, Rotherham

A Sea Poem

The sea is a roaring tiger
Smashing against the shore
It is rippling up and down
More and more
Flowing up the beach
Ebbing its way down
Curving round the rocks in its own way
Eroding rock off the cliffs
Pounding into the flowing sea
The sand is a lovely bed
The sea is a crashing sound
It takes its anger out on the cliffs.

Lauren Bowdler (11)
Blackburn Primary School, Rotherham

The Sea

The sea is calm and really relaxing.
When you're on the beach
You can hear the sea taking
The pebbles and little stones into the sea.
You can hear the sea swaying
And leaping against the rocks and the boulder clay.
A breeze coming over the sea.

Megan Ashall (11)
Blackburn Primary School, Rotherham

A Sea Poem

The smacking, splashing, eating sea
Devouring from the shore
Morsels of sandy food.
That will be more.
The gentle soft tops of the waves
Bring back those happy days
Where creatures crawled here and there
Crabs and lobsters everywhere.

Stephanie Longden (10)
Blackburn Primary School, Rotherham

The Sea

The sea can be a mirror
Reflecting the moon in the darkened skies,
But, don't you trust this beauty
Of treachery and lies.

Because soon it will be
So angry, so angry,
It will crack and split
And take its anger out on the cliffs.
The sea, the sea, the raging sea.

The sea a mirror, no more, no more
Instead, a dragon thrashing its claws,
At last the dragon comes down on all fours
And destroys the houses too near to the shore.

Finally the dragon goes to sleep,
Alone again in its watery deep,
The sea, the sea, no longer will be,
The sea, the sea, the raging sea.

Chris Thompson (11)
Blackburn Primary School, Rotherham

A Sea Poem

The sea roars like a starving lion
The sea spits at Carr Nase which makes the wall crumble.
As it falls down it makes the ground rumble.
It crashes at the rocks.
For people on Filey Brigg it'll sure provide some shocks.
The sea smashes against boats.
The fishermen will be wearing coats.
The sea ebbs out, you can see seven miles of sand.
On the horizon there is a band.
The sea flows to a high tide and licks the shingle.
If you go for a paddle, your feet will tingle.

Adam Kinsella (11)
Blackburn Primary School, Rotherham

A Sea Poem

When the water crashes on the rocks it's beautiful to see,
It's just like something breaking free.
The waves crash and bash onto the seashore,
At the end it's creating more.
The sea smashes against the Carr Nase,
All in many different ways.
As the sea is pounding round,
It's making a whistling sound.
As the boulder clay crumbles,
The loose rock tumbles.
As the waves crash, bash and pound
It still makes all those sounds!

Demi-Leigh Blakesley (11)
Blackburn Primary School, Rotherham

Autumn Poem

The sun has been shining
But in autumn it shines lightly.
Now autumn leaves are falling
Spiders are spinning and crawling
And making pretty webs for us to see each morning.
The sand is sweeping and blowing into our eyes
As fast as people rub their eyes
As fast as they walk past.

Molly Smith (7)
Blackburn Primary School, Rotherham

A Sea Poem

The sea is a calm pup
Slow and soft but sometimes rough.
Windy and rough it can be
Yes, yes, that is the sea.
It crashes and bangs against the cliffs
Causing the rocks to move and shift.
The sea is calm all day
Until it crashes against the boulder clay.
But when it is calm
It won't cause any harm.
Soft and warm waves
In and out the shore all day.
When it is calm it doesn't have its own way
Of crashing against the rocks all day.
Is the sea soft or is it rough?
Eroding the cliffs, it must be tough!

Jessica Hoden (10)
Blackburn Primary School, Rotherham

An Autumn Poem

Here I am, sitting all day
Writing a poem that's coming your way
Trying to win for my school
But I don't know if that is cool
Writing a poem for autumn
Leaves are falling off the trees
Look on the ground and find some keys
Unlock the door to autumn
Conkers fall on your head
Ouch! That hurt, go to bed
Autumn goes, here comes winter
Night, night, Autumn
Hello, Winter.

Sampie Dutka (9)
Burton Leonard CE Primary School, Burton Leonard

Autumn Days

I see the leaves turning day by day
Brown to yellow, then bright orange.
On different trees the conkers fall,
So do the acorns, oh so small.

The leaves are so light, also bright.
But then one day, suddenly, they
Start to crumble, then every different day
They start to lose their colour
And slowly fade away.

Chloe Hemingway (10)
Burton Leonard CE Primary School, Burton Leonard

Lion In The Jungle

Lion in the jungle
Making such a rumble
Panting
In the baking sun.

A pool
The lion drinks
Until he is cool.

A dolphin splashing
Waves crashing
Purple mountains dripping
Gibbons flipping
Through the trees.

Lion in the jungle
The sound of guns
Crashing
Through the trees.

Lion in a cage
The crowd rumbles
As the lion does his tricks.

Clowns splashing
Drums crashing
Purple ice cream dripping
Gymnasts flipping
Through the trapeze.

Lion in the circus
Making no rumble
Panting
In the heat of the tent.

Holly Wilkinson (10)
Eastrington Primary School, Eastrington

The Poem

I've got to write a poem!
But I don't know where to start.
My teacher said I should write it
Straight from the heart.

It's alright for her!
She's done it all before.
But I'm still sat here
Staring at the door.

My friend's writing,
He must have something to do.
I'm sat here thinking,
Staring at my shoe.

The teacher's drinking coffee,
I'm wishing I was home.
I really am no good at this,
It makes me want to groan.

Then suddenly, I've got it!
I could write my feelings down.
Perhaps poetry's not so bad after all,
In fact I'm rather good at it!

Joseph Webster (10)
Eastrington Primary School, Eastrington

Deck That Kid!

'Kill that kid,
Make it hurt.
Kick him down,
Rip his shirt.
Thump his bum,
Make him cry.
Throw a needle in his eye.'

I hear it every day.
But my dad says he'll beat them up
If they don't say sorry.
It's quite funny you know,
Kind of like watching a show.
My dad's really angry with them,
Because they ain't giving in.

Dad's getting quite annoyed
Because they won't shut up.
It's so I have to kill them
And then I'll have to eat them,
But I won't kill them,
I'll walk away,
I'll say no more.
That makes me tougher than them!

Jack Webb (10)
Eastrington Primary School, Eastrington

Miss Daffodilly

Daffodilly, Daffodilly
Turned round and round
A bonnet of goldish-yellow
And a dress of glittery green- brown.
She turned to the west wind and smiled her shining grin
Then turned to the east wind and curtsied up and down.
All this happened on a bright summer's day.
Then the leaves dropped to the glistening ground
And old Miss Daffodilly was nowhere to be found.
As winter lodges in and the warm sun fades out
It's getting colder, without a doubt.
Daffodilly, Daffodilly
A bulb is all that's left
But some day when spring and summer come
Daffodilly will rise more beautiful than before
And everybody will know her for miles and miles around.

Rebecca Watkinson (11)
Eastrington Primary School, Eastrington

Night-Night Teacher

Joy to the world
Our teacher's dead
We finished her off
And barbecued her head.

It wasn't very easy
It was harder than you think
It took a lot of effort
To maker her drink black ink.

But eventually we did it
And she turned a sickly green
She crumpled to the floor
And said that we were mean.

We needed to hide the body
Before the headmaster found it
So we chopped it into pieces
And hid every little bit.

Her arms we put in the big green skip
Her middle we flushed down the loo
Her legs and feet we hid on the field
Then we thought of the barbecue.

Dempsey Walsh (10)
Eastrington Primary School, Eastrington

Circus Lion

I'm in a cramped cage
Until it's my turn to jump the hoop of fire that really burns.
My owners are liars; they say I won't feel pain
But the fire has just started to burn through my mane.

People are clapping and starting to cheer
But I don't like it because it hurts my ear.
I prance and dance around and around
Listening to every sound.

The show is nearly over
So I am finally relieved
I go into my little cage
What have they achieved?

Time for my tiny lunch -
A mouse that runs by.
It goes in just one crunch
And how I want to cry.

So now my day is over
I want to take a nap.
I've done my final dance
I've heard my final clap.

Jasmine Fields-Sanchez (11)
Eastrington Primary School, Eastrington

Untitled

I hate poetry lessons
I don't know why.
I have to write a poem
It makes me want to cry.

She says it is easy,
I think it's really hard.
She's nearly finished
And is mounting it on card!

I haven't even started,
I haven't written a thing!
My friends are all finished,
The bell's about to ring.

Look at the time
The lesson's nearly done.
Whoever said that
Poetry was fun?

Jessica Olsson (10)
Eastrington Primary School, Eastrington

Shipwrecked

I woke up on an island,
I was sure that I had died.
I was alone,
Confused and flustered.
The beating sun burnt my flesh.
The cooling sea lapped my feet.
My dog, my saviour,
Washed up too.
Together we'd come through.
Terrified, panic,
Then sleep.
I woke up on the island
Fresh water at my feet.
Am I alone?

Stephanie Neville (10)
Eastrington Primary School, Eastrington

Shipwrecked

Today I was washed up on a beach.
I found myself with seaweed for feet.
The sand stretched and shimmered as far as I could see,
Beautiful but sad.

Alone, I faced my future.
My life without my friends.
Startling parrots circling above me
And monkeys screeching in my ear.

Azure sea glistening as the sun went down.
Afraid, alone with no one to talk to.
I lay on the sand every night dreaming of my home.

Jessica Mell (10)
Eastrington Primary School, Eastrington

Butterfly

As their wings fly up and down
As they sparkle round and round
As their bright metallic colours
Reflect upon the ground.

As their tiny little faces
Shimmer high above
I watch them from my secret place
I watch them all with love.

As they fly through the crystal sky
And land above my grassy bed
A flutter of more beautiful butterflies
Come flying overhead.

As their petite faces smile
And feelers stand up high
They glide through the air
And make my spirit fly.

Emily Hardcastle (10)
Eastrington Primary School, Eastrington

Teachers

Teachers are such a pain!
They boss you around like they're your mum and dad.
Who do they think they are?
Put on this planet to make me sad.
I sit here day after day
While they get nasty.
I can't wait until 3.30pm, home time.
When it's time for my pasty.
I get in the taxi and then home I go
Just in time for my tea
Or at least I hope so.

George Hall-Lambert (10)
Eastrington Primary School, Eastrington

My Day Fishing

I go fishing by the pond
I sit, I wait, my day seems long
I wait patiently for the fish
To catch my bait
I wait and fish.

I've brought my lunch and tea
Hot tea for Dad
Cold drinks for me.

Dad sits by my side
Helping me when I need it
All day long we sit and wait.

But when the sun is shining on the water
It makes the day seem shorter
When I've nearly had enough
A bubble ripples in the water
I struggle and strain
I land my fish
Dad puts it in the net.

Before too long we've caught a few
And now it's time to let them go
Swim free, little fish
We'll soon be back for more.

Matthew Gribbin (10)
Eastrington Primary School, Eastrington

Through The Sky

I'm crunching through the grass
With my head held high
I just wish I had wings to fly
Like that bird flying in the sky.

And then it happens
My wish comes true
I'm surrounded by clouds
In a sky of blue.

I'm soaring and swooping
And gliding with ease
I'm as light as the wind
Blowing through the trees.

I look down at the fields
I look down at my school
Then I look at my classroom
And know that I'm a fool.

Then I hear the teacher speak
And realise I'm in my class
So it was just in my head
A daydream that couldn't last.

I gaze out through the window
And see the bright blue sky
Then I look back into the classroom
And I have to wonder, *why?*

Beth Graham (10)
Eastrington Primary School, Eastrington

Journey

Today I find myself at sea
With nature for company,
I find myself alone on deck
I think, *I'm surely dead.*

Washed upon a sandy shore
With seaweed at my feet,
A gorgeous island
Dazzling beauty
Parakeets and monkeys.

The sun blazing hot,
Hunger, need food,
Cold water
In a bowl, lots.

I gobble
Relief, such pleasure,
Red bananas, some fish,
Is someone feeding me?
I must find that person, who is he?

I've found this person, is he mad?
I hope that he is not too bad.
I wait for a boat
I want Dad and Mum.

Finally, they've come for me
I've now got them for company.

Charlote Gallagher (10)
Eastrington Primary School, Eastrington

The Poem

I'm heading on a journey
We're going out to sea
My mum and dad are with me.

We see an island in the distance
But the sea becomes really rough
I fall into the deep ocean.

I wake up on the shore
Feeling really scared,
Then I make a fire
Hoping I'll be found.

A man yells and stamps my fire out,
'Dameda, Dameda' I heard.
Then a man stands at my fire,
Who is the person? I wonder.

Where did he come from?
Why is he here?
Will I ever find out?
Will I survive?

Samuel Finelli (10)
Eastrington Primary School, Eastrington

Read Me And Laugh

What to do, I don't have a clue.
Because I did not listen!
We had to write a poem,
But I did not *listen!*
Out to play to find fresh air
But I can't find *any!*
Then back to work,
My brain's melting away
But still I can't *listen!*
It's the end of school,
We're off to the pool to have some *fun!*

Jasmine Daniel (10)
Eastrington Primary School, Eastrington

Shipwrecked

Alone.
Shipwrecked on an island,
Distraught, thinking about my mother and father.
How lonely I was.

Felt a soft, wet tongue lick my face.
All over.
Stella.
My dripping dog, Stella.
We ran.
Out onto the white, glistening sand.
Nearer to the turquoise, sparkling, bubbling sea.
Smoothness.
Lapping against my leg.

One . . . two . . . three!
Jump in.
A cascade of water onto the flat beach.
We lay.
A frothy pool around us.
I turned.
I saw.
A ship.
A ship!
To rescue me!
Slowly.
Very slowly
I turned and waved goodbye.

To the island
Beautiful island
The one that I called mine.

Katie Brophy (10)
Eastrington Primary School, Eastrington

The Teachers

She's kind and caring
Does a lot for me,
She wears those strange half-looking glasses so that she can see.
She sits at her desk with so much marking
But looks up occasionally when people are larking.
When I struggle and get in a fix
She's always there to pick up the bits.
She wears this old grey sweater
That smells like rich perfume.
Her desk is always cluttered
Her mess is taking over the room.
I think she's old and batty, but she's also quite good fun
I think when it's my birthday; I'll bring her a bun
To say thank you!

Ryan Brentville (10)
Eastrington Primary School, Eastrington

The Ocean Wonder

The white sandy beaches
The wide-open shore
The crabs along the beaches
Scuttle along the waves
Fish swim silently
As gulls roar fiercely
The hermits pick up and go
As the driftwood flouts the show
Gibbons guard the palm trees
So predators don't get near
Shells are scattered over the shoreline
The foam of the waves makes a barrier to the beach
Howls from the creatures that live on the island
Echo alone, the white beach creating a place where Man has never set foot
Orang-utans howl to the gibbons
As the wind crows a kingship over everything it sees
Dolphins dance above the waves, showing off their knowledge of gymnastics
Baby whales play with the waves
As their mothers sing to their hearts' content
The sharks rule an undisputed reign over the calm sea
Sea horses race along the coral
The turtles lay their eggs and wait to see how many survive
The waves rear up in rebellion and hit the beach with no repent
The sea glistens as the sun sets over the island beach.

Helen Ashton
Eastrington Primary School, Eastrington

Darkness

When you go into a room where you can't see
And you feel something touching you
Or a spider climbing down your back
You know how a blind man feels walking down a path
What was that at my foot?
Something slithering at my feet
Was that the wall that my hands just touched
Or was that a strange man?
I climb under my covers, safe and warm, away from all my fears.

Jordan McCormack (10)
Malcolm Sargent Primary School, Stamford

Bogeys

There once was a girl called Rose
She loved to pick her nose
She put it in a bucket
And how she loved to suck it!
She owns a great big pot
Full of green snot
Now the pot's gone rusty
The snot's gone crusty.
She had a massive nose bleed
And it looked like seaweed
Rose never picked her nose again
Because of that great nose bleed!

Kerouac Andrews (10)
Malcolm Sargent Primary School, Stamford

Cancer

In ten years' time, far away
There shall be a fantastic day -
All cancer shall disappear
Cured forever, no more fear.
Thousands of people have been petrified
Once told the symptoms of cancer, all have cried.

In ten years' time, far away
There shall be a fantastic day
One day this fearful curse
Shall be treated easily by a nurse.
When this happens, cancer sufferers shall be free,
Hopefully the curer will be me!

Chloe Wells (10)
Malcolm Sargent Primary School, Stamford

PE Teachers

The PE teachers are horrid
They make you stand on your head
Green mats come to life
To gobble little children into their brains
So say you're feeling sick
And never do PE with aliens
Just snuggle up and dream on in bed.

PE is so horrid
Unless it is bench ball
Instead of the five-foot long
Slimy eating mat that chews you up into grit
So never do PE with aliens.

Scott Chamberlain (10)
Malcolm Sargent Primary School, Stamford

A Snail

A snail
Has a shell
Like his home
And when he needs it
He just curls up
And comes out when he needs to.
The only time he comes out is to eat
And that's a snail.

Leo Clarke (10)
Malcolm Sargent Primary School, Stamford

Late For School!

Time is ticking, quick, quick, quick,
Out of bed, brush my teeth.
Get changed, have my breakfast,
Late for the bus, quick, quick, quick!

Mum, brush your teeth, get changed,
Quick, quick, quick!

In the car, hurry, hurry, hurry!
Oh no, school is locked,
Might have to miss school,
Oh no you don't!

I've remembered, it's the summer holidays
No time to lose, go home, I want to play.

Jessica Naylor (10)
Malcolm Sargent Primary School, Stamford

Hallowe'en Holiday

Creepy-crawlies weep
While little children are asleep.

Skeletons sit on toadstools
While witches say, 'This rules!'

Leaves are falling from the trees
While slimy monsters get off their knees.

Dogs and cats and bats and frogs
Maybe even witches' mogs.

Scary noises from that tree
Argh! A beast, it stinks poohy!

Hallowe'en is over now
The witch has left her cat - *miaow!*

Olivia Hibbitt (11)
Malcolm Sargent Primary School, Stamford

A Boy Called Dale

There once was a boy called Dale
Who found a ship and set sail.
He uncovered some trout,
And got pushed out,
And couldn't remember his trail.

Matthew Dowley (10)
Malcolm Sargent Primary School, Stamford

God And The Ink Pen

Today I wrote the Bible
And coloured in the world
Yesterday my ink ran out
While creating all the black holes.
I like to use my ink pen
While writing cool poems
It helps me not go crazy
As I sit up here alone.
I came down as a little kid
To save all of mankind
Oh, my ink's run out, another shopping trip.

Robert Reiss (10)
Malcolm Sargent Primary School, Stamford

Friends

Alice is funny, she always makes me laugh
And the tears we cry of laughter could almost fill a bath.
Charlotte is always there for me when I am upset
But then she reminds me of my pet.
Jessica is one of my best friends, we sometimes fall out
We always make up again and have a laugh and shout.
Mollie is a random person and she is a bit of a wally
She is quite funny and she doesn't like dollies.

All these friends mean something to me
I hope you have friends as special as mine.

Sophie Knox (10)
Malcolm Sargent Primary School, Stamford

All About Cats

Cats are annoying
They always will be.
Cats smell bad
They always will.
Cats need baths
They never will.
Cats need to drink
They never do.
Cats eat lots
They need to.
Cats are out all day
But that's good as we don't have to cope with them.
But most of all, they're cute and cuddly.

Tonicha Bloodworth (10)
Malcolm Sargent Primary School, Stamford

Happiness Is Golden

Happiness is golden
It really has a meaning
Happiness is great
It gives you a good feeling.

You're walking down the street
With a smile on your face
The sun shines brightly
At a perfect pace.

Knowing that the happiness
Is what gives us joy
It gives me happiness
Just playing with a toy.

Charlotte Topping (10)
Malcolm Sargent Primary School, Stamford

Sally The Snake

Sally is a snake.
Oh no, she is awake.
Quick, hide away,
She is getting nearer to our bay.
Sally is green, smooth and soft.
Let's go hide up in our loft.

Run, run, run,
Here she comes.
Oh no, she has got me,
No, I just banged my knee.

Sally the snake slimes and slithers around,
Shhh, be quiet, don't make a sound.
Sally the snake has gone,
We can go to sleep now
And sing Sally a farewell song.
Goodnight everyone!

Charlotte Stygall (10)
Malcolm Sargent Primary School, Stamford

Silence . . .

Silence is a horrible thing
Nothing can be heard
You cannot even hear the sweet chirping of a newborn bird.
Silence feels like you are in the dark
When you may be in the light
How weird, you may be in the dead of night.

Talking is forbidden when silence is around
It's like a bully with silence
Nothing can be found.

In silence you may even feel dread
So what, I just hide under my snug, warm bed.

Nevertheless, one thing is certain
In silence - *shhh*, silence is a cold-hearted demon
Shhh!

Alice Olivia Snell (10)
Malcolm Sargent Primary School, Stamford

Seasons

W ild winter winds wailing
I ncredible forces they give
N arrow rivers freezing over and a
T erribly icy bridge
E veryone keeping warm and
R unning around in woolly clothes

S heep offspring spring to life
P erpetual oak trees shine with life
R ejoicing people fed up with winter
I ndulging in sweet-smelling roses and
N arrow rivers flowing gently and the
G reat sun shimmering from the sea-blue sky

S ummer fruits sweet and juicy
U nder the bridge in the cool, cool river
M ums and dads with their kids cooling off
M idst the river weeds an
E asy life in the cool, cool breeze
R ushing people everywhere heading toward the sea

A pprehensive people annoyed that winter's
U pcoming
T hough the colours of leaves are beautiful
U nruly weather spoils its charm
M any trees are weeping leaves
N ow that winter's here . . .

Olivia Rix (10)
Malcolm Sargent Primary School, Stamford

The Lazy Dragon

The dragon in the cave
Guarding the princess I will save
He's got a very floppy belly
He likes to watch the telly
He breathes lots of fire
He's a big fat liar.

The princess I hear
I ride on a deer
I will always try to save her
I can hear the dragon purr
He's watching cartoons
So I watch the two moons.

The princess will be saved
While the dragon will be bathed
The princess I have saved
The princess will reward me
The princess turned out fine
Tonight, we will dine.

Lewis Edmunds (10)
Malcolm Sargent Primary School, Stamford

Today I'm . . .

Today I'm Jackie Chan
Yesterday I was Elvis Presley
Tomorrow I'll be an angel
Or perhaps a professor.

At morning I'll be a housemaid
At lunch I'll be a chef
At night I'll be a vampire
Spooking all poor souls.

I want to be a millionaire
And save our globe from warming
I want to be a full-time vet
And help all endangered species
Or perhaps I'll have a little break
In front of the telly!

Jonny Evans (10)
Malcolm Sargent Primary School, Stamford

The Black Cat

She's the black cat
She's under my hat
She's quick and sly
She will tell a lie
She walks around the town
She wears the crown
She wins all the bets
She avoids the vets
She is a black jewel
She always rules on Hallowe'en
She is a machine
She is the best
She rides off into the west
She's the best of the best
She rides off into the west.

Samantha Gwinnett (10)
Malcolm Sargent Primary School, Stamford

Time

Time goes
And time flows
Time stays
And time strays.

But every day will turn to night
And darkness will beat the light
Still time will keep on going
Even with you not knowing.

Time goes
And time flows
Time stays
And time strays.

You can never go back to the past
Even if you want it to last
The future will not come to you
Without time passing too.

Time goes
And time flows
Time stays
And time strays.

One day your time will come to an end
And no one will be able to mend
Your unbreathing lungs and unbeating heart
But at the same time a new life will start.

Laura Burney (10)
Malcolm Sargent Primary School, Stamford

Fear Of The Darkness

Darkness, when you go into your room at night
And you put your hand round the corner of the room
Something hits your hand and you run downstairs screaming
But on the way down, fear is following you down the winding stairs.
You tell your dad and you both come and it is haunting you.
When you go into the bedroom, you turn on the light and nothing is there
Apart from my annoying little anxious sister in her bed
Reading to herself and looking like a ghost.

Eleanor Branson (10)
Malcolm Sargent Primary School, Stamford

Horses

Horses are elegant.
Horses can gallop, canter, trot and walk.
Horses have different shades of fur.
There is chestnut gold and chestnut brown.
There is grey or very light blue.
There are different breeds as well.

Some ponies are quite tender.
Some ponies or horses have little sticks or stars on their eyes,
Down to their muzzle.
Some horses are small and stay small.
Some horses are little and will grow very big.
Horses reach up to twenty hands instead of centimetres.
Horses can do jumps up to five foot or a bit more.

Mollie-Mai Earlam (10)
Malcolm Sargent Primary School, Stamford

Socks

I open my drawer and
I see hundreds of socks.
There, waiting for me to
Pull them on my feet.
What socks shall I wear today?

I have shiny socks, long socks,
Short socks, spotty socks, smelly socks,
Itchy socks, comfy socks . . .
Lots of socks!
What socks shall I wear today?

But I do sometimes lose my socks in the wash.
Where do they go?
Who knows!
Maybe to the land of lost socks.
Will I ever get them back?

Gemma Sharman (10)
Malcolm Sargent Primary School, Stamford

Snowboarding

Happiness is when I go snowboarding
When I'm on the slope with friends
When I do challenges and win the newest snowboard
And when I do competitions.

Happiness is when I did the big slope for the first time
When I did the half-pint for the first time.

Now I'm one of the free-riders to do any slope.

Oliver Iredale Hill (10)
Malcolm Sargent Primary School, Stamford

Sadness

S adness is everywhere
A dding darkness to your life
D arkness is above you
N othing to cheer you up
E verything triggers you off
S adness makes you build up your anger
S adness is a part of you.

Sadness is you
What if sadness goes away?
What if sadness stays?
What if sadness is your choice?
What if . . .?

Daniel Gosney (10)
Malcolm Sargent Primary School, Stamford

Alone

Alone for me is missing home,
Forgetting the frosting on a birthday cake,
Falling out with your best friend,
Not lighting the scarlet fire on Christmas Eve.

Being alone is sitting in darkness
And hearing nothing but silence and sly cats on the stone wall outside.
Someone not being there for you
When you scrape your knee or need a hug.

Having no friends and nobody to care about.
Always raining on my parade.
Always cloud, never sun.
Always night, never day.

No pets to look after.
The highlight of life is watching time go by.
Listening to documentaries of world disasters,
Dads travelling away to Iraq and Afghanistan.

Alone is something we all will feel.
But keep with friends
And get out and about
And you'll never be under the curse of alone!

Cara Fountain (11)
Malcolm Sargent Primary School, Stamford

Silence

Silence means nothing, nothing at all
But when you listen
Listen in the darkness
You realise you're not alone.

When the clock ticks and the wind howls
You think you hear a noise
An eerie, ghostly, creaky sound
Something in the moonlit sky.

When the busy day has disappeared
And silence has taken over,
The one thing I don't want is to be alone
Alone in the pitch-black darkness.

Katie Wood (10)
Malcolm Sargent Primary School, Stamford

Darkness

Deep down in the dusty darkness
All is silent, all is quiet.
Nobody to talk to, nothing's there.
Just the moon shining through the night.

Stars glinting in the twilight sky.
Owls hooting and watching you.
Can't see anything, all is black.
The air is cold, I'm cold, everything is cold!

Foxes start pursuing their prey.
Badgers are scrambling around.
Hedgehogs are snuffling for food.
The clock strikes six.

Darkness ends, it's over now
As the sun comes and illuminates the sky.

Arthur Crawford (10)
Malcolm Sargent Primary School, Stamford

Hunger

People starving in the blazing hot desert famine.
Starvation in the sweltering air.
Devastating harvest.
Wells as dry as bones.
Lack of energy, stomach aches, bloated bellies.
Illness, light-headed, starvation in the air.
Death everywhere.
Eagles circling overhead.
Who is alive and who is dead?

Daniel Wade (10)
Malcolm Sargent Primary School, Stamford

My Best Friend

My best friend is Hannah,
She's always there for me,
Although we have our ups and downs,
We're as cheerful as can be.

I can trust my friend,
With almost anything,
She's loving, caring, tender to me,
Oh what joy she brings.

We like to laugh and joke around,
And have a lot of fun,
But when it comes to the serious stuff,
She knows what must be done.

My friend doesn't need a magazine
To tell her what to wear,
She's hip, cool and funky too,
She has a natural flair.

I hope I am as good a friend
As my friend is to me,
Whenever she is down and troubled
She knows where I will be.

Sophie Stafford (10)
Malcolm Sargent Primary School, Stamford

Netball

Netball is so much fun!
Matches are superb.
Tournaments are so energetic.
Setting up for a big match,
C is my favourite position - centre.
With the posts so tall, it's hard to score.
The red and floaty skirts,
I'm glad we've got shorts on underneath!
With the red bibs, it's hard not to be seen.
You've got five seconds to score . . .
Four seconds . . .
Three seconds . . .
Two seconds . . .
One second . . .
Oh no, time up!

Hollie Cummings (10)
Malcolm Sargent Primary School, Stamford

The Noise

I hear a noise downstairs.
I go down with my golf club in case it's a burglar.
I walk down the stairs, there's always a creaky floorboard.
I walk into the kitchen, I turn the light on, I look everywhere but there's no one there.
I turn the light off, I sneak into the dining room but still there's no one there.
Now I give up and I sneak back to bed with a ham sandwich and a packet of crisps.
I fall asleep halfway through eating the crisps.
I wake up again, I hear a turning noise, I go downstairs again with my golf club.
I walk into the spare bedroom but there isn't anyone there except my five cats.
I sigh and think that I will never find out what that noise is.
I think I'll have one more attempt at finding the burglar.
I walk through the doorway into the living room.
First I look around the TV and the chair but nobody is there,
Then I look at the windowsill and the fire but still no one is there, yet again, no burglar.
I sigh and walk out of the room disappointed.
I stop and pull myself together, I walk back in but more confident.
Then I look at the table in the middle of the room
I hear the turning noise again, this time louder.
I see the so-called burglar, he is . . .
My hamster running madly on his running wheel!

Alex Engel (10)
Malcolm Sargent Primary School, Stamford

Netball

Netball is fantastic!
I usually shoot and score
Then my friend goes and shoots
But this time we had bad luck.
Even though we won 3-0
We kept passing and we had to play fast.
We were all squirming through the other team .

Jessica Marshall (10)
Malcolm Sargent Primary School, Stamford

Skiing

Skiing to go rapidly down the steep slope
Boots to clip into skis
Poles push down the snow
Cosy gloves to keep my hands warm
Warm hat to protect my head.

Abigail Wilson (10)
Malcolm Sargent Primary School, Stamford

Happiness Is Sweet

Happiness is when you play with your friends.
Happiness is when your teacher praises you.
Happiness is when your mum hugs you.
Happiness is when you're snug and warm in bed.
Happiness is when you're watching an excellent TV programme.
Happiness is when you're working extremely hard.
Happiness is when you're helping your brothers.
Happiness is when you're playing with your brothers.
Happiness is when you're playing with your fluffy pet.
Happiness is when you're playing in the garden.

My dad's happy when he gets a hug.
My mum's happy when I do well at school.
My brother, William's happy when he scores.
My brother, George is happy when he rides his bike.
My grandma's happy when she sees gorgeous me.
My grandad's happy when I help him.
My teacher's happy when my work's good.
I'm happy when everyone's happy.

James Germany (10)
Malcolm Sargent Primary School, Stamford

Watching You

Heart bashing hard, eyes watching you
Everything you do
They are watching you
So scared you can't move
You think it's going smooth
But it's not because they are watching you
Even putting on your shoes
You see, the eyes love watching you, spying you
So watch out because they could be watching everything you do
They'll be watching you.

Chloe Hodge (11)
Malcolm Sargent Primary School, Stamford

Alone

Sitting down in an empty corridor,
Alone . . .
Nobody knows how I feel.
Scared and alone in a dark, dark corner,
Alone . . .
But wait!
Here comes a light in the dark!
Someone has come into this dark corridor
And his name is . . .
Courage.

Laurie Rae (10)
Malcolm Sargent Primary School, Stamford

Happiness

Happiness is sport for me.
Happiness is cricket for me.
Happiness is hockey for me.
Happiness is football for me.
Happiness is squash for me.
Happiness is running for me.
Happiness is basketball for me.
Happiness is rugby for me.
Happiness is skiing for me.
So sport is important for me.

Happiness is playing for me.
Happiness is school for me.
Happiness is art for me.
Happiness is maths for me.
Happiness is PE for me
But my favourite thing of all would have to be my friends.

Zak Chappell (10)
Malcolm Sargent Primary School, Stamford

The Owl

In the dark and dusty forbidden forest
Where the owl toots its daring hoot
Every night when we try to rest
All we hear is the owl's hoot.

In the darkness you see its eyes glowing like stars
The owl whooshes through mid-air like dust
It flies around looking for prey
When the animals hear this, they know they're OK.

The owl has warm, smooth, black fur
He roams around following his nose
He zooms across the water's edge
Like a kingfisher looking for fish.

Zak Warrener (10)
Malcolm Sargent Primary School, Stamford

Darkness

When it's dusk everything goes quiet, just think . . .
There are planets swirling around in the night's sky
Just sitting on the grass verge looking at the stars
Sometimes you might see a shooting star
And just think, there might be a man on that moon tonight!

Squirming, jumping, digging
All the animals splodging in the mud in the darkness
All you can see are things bouncing on the floor
The rabbits hopping elegantly, the frogs bouncing high.

Lauren Bolster (10)
Malcolm Sargent Primary School, Stamford

Chocolate

Toffee, caramel, white, dark
I love chocolate!
One nibble, to one bite,
To one mouthful, to one bar,
Mmmm! So succulent!

As you eat, a creamy taste spreads
Across your tongue.
Caramel, sticky,
Toffee, tasty!

In the sweet shop
Not knowing what to have -
Yorkie, Aero, Kit-Kat, all so delicious!
Which one to choose . . .
Hang on, I know . . .
Have the lot!

Joseph Begley (10)
Malcolm Sargent Primary School, Stamford

The Creature

The misty grey clouds resting upon me
The bitter wind echoing in my ears
Sounding like ghostly screams
The piercing silence making the world seem dead,
I see it . . .
I see a face so deadly and painful
A sudden thirst runs down my throat
I could die within these injurious seconds
Neither I nor you could face the blood-curdling appearance of the . . .

Charlotte Neal (10)
Malcolm Sargent Primary School, Stamford

Love

When we first met I had butterflies in my tummy.
I smelt of fresh roses from the garden.
I saw people kissing with presents in their hands.
I wished I was them.

Dana Hooper (10)
Malcolm Sargent Primary School, Stamford

Anger

The bang of exploding grenades, the boom of the war hammer
Crashing down on the enemy skull.
The colour of dark blue, of ultramarine armour
And the taste of blood splattered across the armour,
The smell of flesh as bullets tear through.
It reminds me of the Grim Reaper levitating across the field taking lives.

Kieran Williams (11)
Malcolm Sargent Primary School, Stamford

Fear

Walking down that fearful street
I hum a little tune from a horror movie.
I suddenly stop and listen . . .
In the darkness of the distance
I hear a loud, piercing sound coming from in front of me.
Then I feel a shiver down my spine;
Without looking behind me, I run.
Run!
Run!
I stop to the taste of vomit running down my stiff throat.
I look around me . . .
All I can see is red blood dripping from everything.

Alyssa Henry (10)
Malcolm Sargent Primary School, Stamford

ppy children, laughter in the park.
ng bubble wrap after unwrapping a present.
The pink chocolate taste like strawberry.

Kolmol Przystupa (10)
Malcolm Sargent Primary School, Stamford

Love

The sound of kissing with the smell of laughter in the background.
The feel of fresh peaches and the look of hearts
That have a colour of red that reminds you of red roses.

Samuel Wood (10)
Malcolm Sargent Primary School, Stamford

Sadness, Happiness And Hope!

The sound of lightning echoed through the sky
Shadowing me with its dark, gloomy wings.
Sadness struck me sharply, darkly,
I could not get away.

But what was coming over the horizon?
It was a small bird.
It was happiness, it was hope.
It was glowing lightly, brightly.
I didn't want to go away.
First I felt sadness with its shadowy wings.
Then I felt hope with the happiness it brings.

Charlotte Black (10)
Malcolm Sargent Primary School, Stamford

Silence

Silence, it appears as if everything is hidden
Under a veil of black darkness.
The taste of nothing combined with the sound of suspense.
Silence, it feels as if you are being frozen from the inside out
And the smell of stale, rotting cabbage.
Silence, the thought of empty nothingness.

Liam Claughton (10)
Malcolm Sargent Primary School, Stamford

Darkness

The clouds of smoke make you cough and splutter.
The midnight sky is vile and sickening.
Smooth as pebbles in the water.
Shrieks coming from young children seeping under the floorboards.

Hannah Long (10)
Malcolm Sargent Primary School, Stamford

Silence

The sound of a graveyard echoes around paper.
Feels like nothing coming our way.
The smell of freshwater travelling up your nose
The whiteness of day lives on forever!

Hannah Freshwater (10)
Malcolm Sargent Primary School, Stamford

Love And Hate

Lovely red roses
The colour of cherries
Feels as soft as baby-pink
Lovely scented flowers
Seems so nice, they look like hearts!

Sadness filling all the Earth
Something hard like the ground
Hearing crying every day
Red, red blood you picture in your mind
Dripping like ice cubes with the smell of mouldy bread
The crying carries on, trapped in your mind forever.

Anya Evitts (10)
Malcolm Sargent Primary School, Stamford

Anger

The colour of you is like a red-hot chilli pepper in a 500^0 oven!
You can taste a bolt of lightning about to come out of your mouth!
The smell is the most ghastly smell of wine (which is out of date) and sick!
You look like a dark red volcano about to explode,
Getting bigger and bigger every half second!
You feel like a demented hippo with a feeling like a constipated cat!
It will remind you of getting out of bed and screaming and swearing,
It also smells like gasoline.

William Pearce (10)
Malcolm Sargent Primary School, Stamford

Anger

Walking round and round in circles
Anger pouring out of my brain
And the colour red filling my eyes
The bitter taste dribbles through my mouth
The bellowing of noises through day and night
Children crying, it becomes a fright
Looking at the sharp spikes spinning in your mind
Then all of a sudden they're grinding down my spine
Smells of rotten flesh and meat covered in hay
The lack of sleep sweeping through my brain
I think it's trying to play like a game.

Jack Bishop (10)
Malcolm Sargent Primary School, Stamford

Love

As a pink love heart appears
A couple of love doves swoop to the love tree
The taste of strawberries goes down
As the smell of sweet perfume spreads through the air
As you walk through the scented smell you see the person that is made for you
And you bond together to create a new person
As the birds sing as they soar through the air.

Joe Czornookyj (10)
Malcolm Sargent Primary School, Stamford

Anger

Anger is rough,
Makes you feel tough.
You roar as loud as a lion,
Your face goes all red,
You jump on your bed,
And cry for the rest of the day.

You wake the next day,
You feel OK,
You've forgotten about yesterday.

Michael Sims (10)
Malcolm Sargent Primary School, Stamford

It's Uncontrollable

It's uncontrollable, it's uncontrollable.
You just can't stop it!
As wars are about you and murders take place,
You're going up in flames with anger!
As lava belches oily blood from rotting flesh, the smell goes rushing up your nose.

It's uncontrollable, it's uncontrollable.
Don't try to resist.
As the school bully pushes you about, trying to scare you.
When you start to feel the crimson flames of the oven that's been on for twenty hours
Then you turn around and shout, 'Stop!'
He is clearly shocked.

Connor Rawnsley (10)
Malcolm Sargent Primary School, Stamford

Happiness

Like sugar swirling around in your mouth,
Like birds singing songs in harmony
On a warm summer day with a pleasant warm breeze.
A couple of swallows darting round as they're playing tig.
The smell of yellow candyfloss being spun into a light,
Fluffy bundle of sugar.
With small guinea pigs doing a funny little jump against a wall
Under the bright yellow sunshine, gleaming down to Earth.

Megan Komoto (10)
Malcolm Sargent Primary School, Stamford

Silence

Silence, waiting for something to split the air
Black, nothingness, darkness, no colour, blank.
Waiting, waiting, there are butterflies in my stomach
Something must be wrong.
Waiting, waiting, total isolation, nothing to do, see or hear.
Abandoned in the wilderness.
Waiting, waiting, hoping, hoping, dreaming.

Christina Farmbrough (11)
Malcolm Sargent Primary School, Stamford

Darkness

Black as midnight
It creeps up on me
I hear a creak
Turn sharply and see
Nothing
Was it real
Or was I imagining it?
I keep walking
But a dry and sickly taste
Spreads in my mouth
Trapped, no escape
I feel a chill
A deadly chill
Run up my spine
And whenever I take another step
I see a figure
In the corner of my eye.

Sarah Burley (10)
Malcolm Sargent Primary School, Stamford

Love

Love is like seeing two doves singing in a tree.
It makes your cheeks go red like a love heart.
It tastes like a romantic meal.
It smells like fresh air in a field full of roses.
It reminds you of your past love life.
Love feels like a great world made better, like a new life.
It sounds like the laughter of a happy couple.

Robert Knight (10)
Malcolm Sargent Primary School, Stamford

The Zoo

I went to the strangest zoo
With the kangaraff and the elepharoo
And don't forget the tigerpotamus too!
But none of those are as daft
As the hyena-aff!
But sadly now I have to leave
And go to see my dogish cat, Steve.

Alice Pridham (9)
Scotter Primary School, Gainsborough

The Cheetah

Big round ears
Delicate and soft
Always alert
Always picking up sounds.

Thin golden eyes
Sparkly and light
Always watching
Always staring off into the distance.

Long furry tail
Slim and beautiful
Always twitching
Always balancing himself.

Long slender legs
Thin and strong
Always running
Always pumping blood.

Big soft paws
Cushiony and padded
Always moving
Always thudding against the ground.

Beautiful spotty coat
Shiny and thick
Always beautiful
Always blending into the background.

Kelly Welch (10)
Scotter Primary School, Gainsborough

My Special Holiday

Off to Cyprus in the sun,
Hoping to have lots of fun.
Welcome to the island of dreams
Ice creams! Ice creams! Ice creams!

I'll sunbathe in the sun,
I'll splash around in the sea,
I'll play in the sand
Oh, that's so lovely for me.
Ice creams! Ice creams! Ice creams!

Swimming pools are my delight,
Splashing, playing, water fight?
Back to the beach to have more fun
Relaxing under the sun.
Snorkelling for shells, rocks and sea cucumber,
Such a nice place of magical wonder.
The sun is strong, I shade my eyes
Now it's time for a surprise!
Ice creams! Ice creams! Ice creams!

When it's dark and night-time
It's time for food and time to dine
Feta salad, kebabs and shish,
Pork chops, halloumi, meze and fish
All sorts of fruit and Cyprus delight
Make many, many, many late nights.
Ice creams! Ice creams! Ice creams!

Goodbye, goodbye, the time has come
To board that plane away from the sun.
I go to bed and dream and dream and dream
No more ice creams! Ice creams! Ice creams!
My island of dreams, dream, dreams!

Lucy McGrath (8)
Scotter Primary School, Gainsborough

My Autumn

Autumn is here now, apples and berries,
Conkers and acorns too
Bonfire Night and Remembrance Day,
Hallowe'en, harvest, hip hip *hooray!*
Autumn is here now,
Nights grow darker, days are shorter,
I can't go out to play.
Farmers are cutting crops to store.
Autumn is here now,
It's getting colder, big coats on.
Rain and umbrellas too
Fires on reds and yellows, *keep warm!*
Autumn is here now.

Hannah Mayall (9)
Scotter Primary School, Gainsborough

Picky

Picky is my pony's name,
He likes me brushing his chestnut mane.
I like to walk him down the lane.

I like to clean his little feet
And give him Polos as a treat.

When he sees me he seems to say
Hello! by giving me a little neigh.

Tuesday Whybrow (8)
Scotter Primary School, Gainsborough

Monkey

M unching on squishy bananas
O pening his eyes, peeking at me
N imbly swinging from tree to tree
K arate chopping their branches
E nergetically chasing his playmates
Y elling excitedly, 'Tig, you're it!'

Lauren Thompson (9)
Scotter Primary School, Gainsborough

Along The Beach

Waves are blue and crash,
When you jump in them they splash.
The beach is covered with pebbles and sand,
When my father grabs me by the hand,
We walk along collecting shells
Then I hear the ringing bells.
It's time to go home for tea,
All together we shall be.

Olivia Foster (7)
Scotter Primary School, Gainsborough

Kennings

Black and white
Cold and tight
Can't fly
Might try
Ice-slider
Snow-glider
Fish-eater
Arctic-seater
Polar bear hater
Black-and-white waiter
Lives in water
Can't get hotter
A cute penguin on ice.

Callum O'Rourke (10)
Scotter Primary School, Gainsborough

Creatures In My Garden

Worms and snails and little green frogs
Wriggling woodlice under the logs
Beautiful blackbirds building a nest
Never seen having a rest.

Whizzing wasps and buzzing bees
Hiding in the leafy trees
Crawling ladybirds shiny and red
Trying to find a spotty bed.

But something is very scary
And very, very hairy.
I don't know what it is
It must be a . . .
Spider!

Beth Good (7)
Scotter Primary School, Gainsborough

Cats

Some cats are big and some cats are small
They land on their feet when they fall.
They sleep all day and play all night.
You can even hear them having a fight.
They hunt for birds and run after mice
Now that can't be nice!

Gemma Talbot (8)
Scotter Primary School, Gainsborough

My Early Morning Visit To Nan's Coffee Shop

Bacon on the grill, sausages sizzling, eggs splattering,
It smells delicious and my mouth's watering.
Scones are rising in the oven,
Ready to be sold by the dozen.
The kettles are on the boil and the coffee is percolating.
The milkshake machine (mmm, my favourite) is frothing.
Now it's almost time to open.
Oops, someone's forgotten to defrost the pie from frozen.
Staff are chatting when they should be working.
What will Nan say when she sees them not cooking?
The manageress is getting all stressed out
I think my nan's about to shout.
The first customers of the day are here,
They think a breakfast is a bit too dear!
They say, can they have a cup of tea
Oh no, I think, *they are asking me!*
'I'm only ten - don't ask me - I can't do it,' I say!
Oh good, they're going away - *hooray!*

Katy Langley (10)
Scotter Primary School, Gainsborough

The Writer Of This Poem

(Based on 'The Writer of this Poem' by Roger McGough)

Is as strong as a tiger,
As gentle as a daisy,
As fast as a leopard,
As slow as a snail,
As happy as Mr Dark,
As silly as a dog,
As busy as a bee,
As cold as an ice cube,
As graceful as a dolphin,
And as pretty as the sun.

Gabriella Whybrow (9)
Scotter Primary School, Gainsborough

Competition

I want to win a thousand pounds.
For my school today.
They said I had to write a poem
But they didn't say which way.
I wrote it on the toilet
I wrote it on the bus
I tried to write it in my bed
But Mum just made a fuss.
My teacher said it had to be
'Just right and not too long'
Not like some of those boring poems
That go on and on and on.
So here it is . . .
It was a dark and dreary night
The toilet light was dim
I heard a crash and then a splash
Oh no, he's fallen in!

Tom Sampson (8)
Scotter Primary School, Gainsborough

What Is A Cat?

Gentle eyes that see so much
Paws that have the quiet touch.
Purrs to signal all is well
And shows more love than words can tell.
Graceful movements touched with pride
A calming presence by our side.
A friendship that will last and grow
Small wonder why we love them so.

Charlene Wilcock (8)
Scotter Primary School, Gainsborough

Autumn

Autumn days
Sunny ways
Clouds dark
Singing lark
Empty streets
Television repeats
Falling leaves
Hot sleeves.

Stephen Cox (10)
Scotter Primary School, Gainsborough

Tomatoes

Big ones, little ones,
Red ones, yellow ones,
They come in all shapes and sizes
And can be full of surprises.
You grow them in your garden,
I beg your pardon?
Tomatoes, of course
They make a beautiful sauce.

Emily Crosby (8)
Scotter Primary School, Gainsborough

Yellow

Yellow is the sun, shining bright
Yellow is a butterfly ever so light.
Yellow is a buttercup swaying in the grass
Yellow is the name of the table in my class.

Beth Montgomery (8)
Scotter Primary School, Gainsborough

The Sparkling Light Of The Sea

When the sun shines, the sea starts to glitter
I feel harmony in my heart.
I feel safe from my fear
I look around and feel at home but I'm not.
I'm standing on the sand all soft around my feet
The wind blows and the sand swirls around in a circle.

Lauren Nicholls (9)
Scotter Primary School, Gainsborough

Oh No, I've Forgotten . . .

Oh no, I've forgotten my spelling book,
Whatever shall I do?
It's my spelling test today
What is my teacher going to say?

Oh no, I've forgotten my PE kit,
Whatever shall I do?
I want to keep as fit as I can
And grow into a healthy man.

Oh no, I've forgotten my raincoat,
Whatever shall I do?
It's going to rain, I know it will
I hope that I don't catch a chill.

Oh no, I've forgotten it's Saturday,
Whatever shall I do?
I'm out of bed and ready for school
I feel just like a great big fool!

I've made a promise to myself
So I won't feel so rotten.
What's the promise that I made?
Oh no, I've forgotten!

Kirk Owst (8)
Scotter Primary School, Gainsborough

Hallowe'en Spooks Night

Spooky costumes, apple bobbing and trick or treats
Lots of lovely things to eat.

Scary pumpkin faces lit with candlelight
Flickering lanterns burning bright.

Something waiting, waiting to scare
Dark shadows everywhere.

Strange shapes creep up from the damp ground
Hiding in the mist swirling around.

Silently waiting for you to appear
Then as soon as they scare you they disappear.

Shhh! Night- night, sleep tight
Don't worry, it will soon be light.

Bethany Marshall (9)
Scotter Primary School, Gainsborough

Macbeth

Two and twenty beetles' eyes
Add a rat of no great size.
The babe of a lion, the tail of a snake
The scale of a beast from Nessie's lake.
Leg of a dragonfly,
Hairs from the fox so sly.
Nails of a witch, still in her youth
And a curse that cometh from Satan's mouth.
Finish it off with one and sixty stirs
And tell the future for he and her.

'Double, double, toil and trouble
Fire burn and cauldron bubble.'

Gaia Fay Lambert (10)
Scotter Primary School, Gainsborough

A Funny Poem

I wanted to write a good rhyme,
With humour, slapstick and mime.
It had to be funny,
To make lots of money
But sorry, I didn't have the time!

Thomas Bywood (11)
Scotter Primary School, Gainsborough

Autumn

Autumn
Crispy leaves
Children wearing coats
It's time to celebrate
Harvest.

Holly Girven (9)
Scotter Primary School, Gainsborough

At The End Of The School Assembly

Mr Bumble's lot buzzed off
Miss Storm's lot thundered out
Mrs Jumper's lot hopped out
And Mr Fashions's lot strutted out.

Miss Ball's lot rolled out
Mr Baby's lot crawled out
Miss Clumsy's lot clambered out
And Mrs Brook's lot simply trickled away.

Becky Evans (9)
Scotter Primary School, Gainsborough

Autumn

Autumn is brown like leaves of an old tree.
It tastes like apples dipped in chocolate.
It sounds like conkers falling to the ground.
It looks like fireworks booming in the sky.
It smells like sizzling sausages.
It makes me feel smiley.

James Oxley (7)
Shooters Grove Primary School, Sheffield

Autumn

Autumn is dark and brown.
It tastes like chewy apples and lovely candy.
It sounds like rustling leaves.
It looks like a sausage sandwich cooking.
It smells like colourful fires in the moonlight.
It makes me feel happy and pleased.

Megan McAllister (8)
Shooters Grove Primary School, Sheffield

Autumn

Autumn is beautiful and exciting.
It tastes like bubbly hot soup and toffee apple.
It sounds like leaves crunching and crackling.
It looks like fireworks and banging.
It smells like hot chocolate and it smells great.
It makes me feel jolly and happy.

Emily Balderstone (7)
Shooters Grove Primary School, Sheffield

Autumn

Autumn is joyful and happy.
It tastes like hot candy being toasted.
It sounds like crunching leaves.
It looks like dazzling fireworks.
It smells like fresh leaves.
It makes me feel very glad.

Kate Hogg (7)
Shooters Grove Primary School, Sheffield

The Amazing Rainforest

It is amazing.
That animal is dashing.
I think someone's hunting.
Look at that pig, it's grunting.
Has it lost its mummy?

It's vanishing,
People are leaving,
I think the tribe has gone,
I am the only one
Who has not disappeared

It's lovely.
It's lovely and jolly.
The tribe is back,
Now. let's have a party!

It's going to be great
We'll invite all our mates,
The animals too,
I really can't wait!

It's a real big shame,
This amazing place
Is vanishing.

Zoe Lindley (9)
Shooters Grove Primary School, Sheffield

The Jungle

Morning's here like a flow,
The animals are on the go.
People stalking on the hunt,
Hungry gorillas having a grunt!
Animals are under threat,
Whilst being trapped in a net!
The fish are caught by a spear,
While men make sure the coast is clear!

Time to sleep in the jungle,
Animals stop having a rumble.
Come together in a huddle,
All the animals have a cuddle.
Night-time here once again,
Lions sleeping in their den.

Nicola Smith (9)
Shooters Grove Primary School, Sheffield

Animals Of The Rainforest

(Inspired by 'Waiting' by Richard Blythe)

Look out, there are predators creeping,
Jaguars leaping,
Silly ones swinging,
Big monkeys singing,
The animals of the jungle.

The trees are coming down,
Bushbabies are wearing a frown,
The snakes are slithering around,
The animals of the jungle.

The frogs are jumping,
Alligators out of bounds,
The people are making weird sounds,
The animals of the jungle.

Leopards are coming for you,
They don't live in a zoo,
The people are hunting,
Gorillas are grunting,
The animals of the jungle.

Nicholas Hill (10)
Shooters Grove Primary School, Sheffield

They're On The Way For Me!

Shhh! says the snake wrapping round a tree.
He stops!
He looks!
And he's on the way for me.

Roar! goes the tiger, stalking for his prey!
He stops!
He looks!
And I'm sure he's on the way.

Squawk! goes that parrot that just ate a flea!
He stops!
He looks!
And he's on the way for me!

The snake, the lion, the parrot and me
And, oh yes
That poor helpless little flea.
What have I done? What have I done?
They're all on the way for me!

Thomas Bower (9)
Shooters Grove Primary School, Sheffield

The Rainforest

The snakes are slithering in the forest,
He is creeping for the animals,
Every bird is flapping in the sky,
Rustling in the trees,
The monkeys swing from tree to tree.
The forest loves the tiger.
Night-time animals are creeping.
The forest floor is there.
The otter is swimming in the water.
Rainforests are full of animals.
Every leopard is looking for food
Swinging from the trees upside down.
The parrots are colourful.

Lauren Whitehead (9)
Shooters Grove Primary School, Sheffield

Jungle Rap

There's a rumble in the jungle,
There's a whisper in the trees,
Animals are waking up
And rustling in the leaves.
Jaguars are stretching,
Armadillos fetching,
Crocodiles hunting down their prey!
There's a silence in the jungle,
There's a whisper in the trees,
Animals are sleeping now
There's no rustling in the leaves.
Lions sleeping in their dens,
Cubs dozing in their pens,
Animals rustling close and near
Day has gone, now night is here, *shhh!*

Courtney Claxton (9)
Shooters Grove Primary School, Sheffield

Autumn

Autumn is very colourful, golden and yellow
Falling leaves on the ground
It tastes like a toffee apple.
It sounds like fireworks crackling in the sky.
It looks like fireworks booming in the sky.
It smells like sizzling sausages in the pan.
It makes me feel pleased and jolly.

Will Travis (7)
Shooters Grove Primary School, Sheffield

Autumn

Autumn is colourful and crispy.
It tastes like sizzling sausages in an oven.
It sounds like birds tweeting in the breeze.
It looks like sparkling fireworks.
It smells like burnt toffee and boiling tea.
It makes me feel delighted and blithe.

Hannah Letts (7)
Shooters Grove Primary School, Sheffield

Autumn

Autumn is very cold and windy.
It tastes like sizzling sausages.
It sounds like crunching leaves.
It looks like a big leaf falling from a tree.
It smells like a runny, sticky orange.
It makes my feet very glad and smiley.

Annabel Limb (7)
Shooters Grove Primary School, Sheffield

Autumn

Autumn is yellow and brown, bright orange, golden.
It tastes like beans on toast and pie.
It sounds like crunching leaves and wind.
It looks like bare trees and leaves falling off the trees.
It makes me feel happy, excited and jolly.

Shania Bates (7)
Shooters Grove Primary School, Sheffield

Autumn

Autumn is golden, red and bright orange.
It tastes like burnt toast and warm beans.
It sounds like whistling wind and crunching leaves.
It looks like a bare place with leaves flying.
It smells like burning bonfires at night-time.
It makes me feel warm and cosy.

George Johnson (7)
Shooters Grove Primary School, Sheffield

Autumn

Autumn is brawny and yellow.
It tastes like buttery toast and warm soup.
It sounds like crunchy leaves falling from the trees
and leaves on the floor.
It smells like Bonfire Night with toffee apples.
It makes me feel warm and happy.

Millicent Renshaw (7)
Shooters Grove Primary School, Sheffield

Autumn

Autumn is red and yellow.
It tastes like bubbling stew.
It sounds like the crunching of the leaves.
It looks like bare trees.
It smells like bonfires.
It makes me feel like fireworks.

Jack Clithero Barrett (7)
Shooters Grove Primary School, Sheffield

Autumn

Autumn is reddy, purple and orange.
It tastes like crunchy apple pie and bramble pie.
It sounds like crunchy leaves and people's voices.
It looks like bare cold trees and brown leaves.
It smells like lovely golden syrup.
It makes me feel warm in my own bed.

Georgia Goodman (7)
Shooters Grove Primary School, Sheffield

Autumn

Autumn is golden yellow and dark brown.
It tastes like sugary pancakes with mushroom soup and bread.
It sounds like squashed leaves blowing against the brick houses.
It smells like sizzling sausages cooking on a bonfire.
It makes me feel happy and excited in the cold autumn days in the tropical winds.

Imogen Southern (7)
Shooters Grove Primary School, Sheffield

Autumn

Autumn is yellowy-brown and golden-red.
It tastes like bubbling hot soup with bread.
It sounds like wind blowing the trees from side to side.
It looks like bare trees and leaves everywhere.
It smells like fish and chips to warm people up.
It makes me feel super-duper happy and special.

Luke Marsh (7)
Shooters Grove Primary School, Sheffield

Autumn

Autumn is dark purple and manky yellow.
It tastes like chocolate chip cookies.
It sounds like the wind rustling in the breeze.
It looks like bonfires burning in the night.
It smells like daisies in the meadows.
It makes me feel snug.

Hannah Whelan (7)
Shooters Grove Primary School, Sheffield

What Is A Fig?

A fig is a purpley pink colour.
It tastes gorgeous.
It smells fantastic.
It feels squidgy,
It looks like a purple onion.
It reminds me of my dad.

Shannon Griffiths (7)
Shooters Grove Primary School, Sheffield

Autumn

Autumn is golden-yellow and yellow-red.
It tastes like beans on toast and hot stew.
It sounds like crunching leaves from the fall.
It looks like dull trees with leaves in the air.
It smells like burning wood from the seas.
It makes me feel happy and jolly and it makes me feel that I was there.

Joseph Ashworth (7)
Shooters Grove Primary School, Sheffield

Autumn

Autumn is brawny, gold and bright orange.
It tastes like hot, lovely stew.
It sound like crunching leaves blowing in the air.
It looks like a sunny autumn day.
It smells like burning toast in the oven.
It makes me feel happy and cold in my bed.

Haris Luxton-Brookes (7)
Shooters Grove Primary School, Sheffield

Autumn

Autumn is browny and orange-red.
It tastes like stew and beans.
It looks like leaves in the sky.
It sounds like leaves in the wind.
It smells like pie and bacon.
It makes me feel happy and warm.

Jack Hill (7)
Shooters Grove Primary School, Sheffield

Autumn

Autumn is brown-red and crispy brown.
It tastes like a salty chip butty followed by nice hot apple pie.
It sounds like children's laughter on a creepy night.
It looks like falling down trees with colourful leaves blowing in the breeze.
It smells like a bonfire burning my Sunday lunch mixed with wood.
It makes me have a lovely warm feeling inside.

Lucy Bower (7)
Shooters Grove Primary School, Sheffield

Autumn

Autumn is yellowy and shiny red.
It tastes like bubbling stew and juicy apple pie.
It sounds like crunching leaves under my feet.
It looks like bare trees and leaves flying in the air.
It smells like gas blowing around and burning wood.
It makes me feel nice and all snuggled up in bed.

Charlie King (8)
Shooters Grove Primary School, Sheffield

Autumn

Autumn is golden, orange and brown.
It tastes like hot lasagne and nice spicy soup.
It sounds like fireworks and crackling bombs.
It looks like nice rivers sailing along.
It smells like burning bombs screaming in the air.
It makes me feel excited and happy.

Max Vickers (7)
Shooters Grove Primary School, Sheffield

Autumn

Autumn is golden, browny red and yellow.
It tastes like beans on toast and hot, juicy, squirting pie.
It sounds like crunching leaves and wind whistling.
It looks like bold trees and green lovely grass.
It smells like bonfire sticks and leafy woods.
It makes me feel cosy, warm and excited.

Rose Forster (7)
Shooters Grove Primary School, Sheffield

Autumn

Autumn is browny and red and bright orange.
It tastes like hot pizza and lovely sweet lasagne.
It sounds like rockets and sparklers.
It looks like bare trees and crunchy leaves.
It smells like bonfires and rockets.
It makes me feel happy and jolly.

Holly Gregory (7)
Shooters Grove Primary School, Sheffield

Autumn

Autumn is rosy red and bright orange.
It tastes like apple pie with cream and bubbling bacon.
It sounds like crunchy leaves and conkers falling off the trees.
It looks like flashing, twirling bombs in the sky.
It smells like burnt wood and roaring fires.
It makes me feel cosy and warm when I snuggle up in my bed.

Georgina Horton (7)
Shooters Grove Primary School, Sheffield

Autumn

Autumn is golden-red and brown, leafy.
It tastes like hot buttery soup.
It sounds like crunching leaves on the ground.
It looks like leaves are falling from the sky.
It smells like the breeze around me.
It makes me feel jolly, happy and warm.

Charlotte Holmes (7)
Shooters Grove Primary School, Sheffield

Weather Days

Summer sun is golden-yellow
While the rain is fresh and clear
Clouds are white and fluffy
And rainbows are just pretty.

Lightning can be scary
Thunder can make me jump
Snow can be made into balls
And hailstones just hurt.

Fog you can't see through
Mist is only thin
The moon glows very bright
And lights up everything.

The wind is really breezy
Snowflakes come in different shapes
Stars are bright and sparkly
And shine all night.

Alexandra Snape (9)
Woodmansey CE Primary School, Beverley

Animal Alphabet

A is for ant
B is for bear
C is for cat
D is for dolphin
E is for elephant
F is for fish
G is for goat
H is for horse
I is for iguana
J is for jack rabbit
K is for kangaroo
L is for lizard
M is for monkey
N is for newt
O is for owl
P is for parrot
Q is for quail
R is for rats
S is for seal
T is for tortoise
U is for urchin
V is for vole
W is for whale
X is for xanu
Y is for yak
Z is for zebra.

Arcadia Yeats (10)
Woodmansey CE Primary School, Beverley

My Garden

My garden is the best,
That's where I have a rest.
It's full of beautiful colours,
Green, blue, brown and white.
I look at them with all my might,
What a wonderful sight.

My garden is very big,
On the ground there will be a twig.
The birds will make a nest,
My garden is the best.
The flowers will grow
Out of the ground below.
That's why my garden is the best.

Charlotte Daw (10)
Woodmansey CE Primary School, Beverley

Spider Began

(Inspired by 'Cat Began' by Andrew Matthews)

He took the rope from a net
He took the honey from the cone
And made his sticky web.

For his eyes
He took a number of Millions
He snatched the roundness of a ball.

From the deadliness of the killer bee
He took the sting
He took the fangs of the cobra
And they were for his venom.

At night he took
The blackness of the trees' branches
The point of an old fishing hook
And made his legs.

Daniel Los (8)
Woodmansey CE Primary School, Beverley

Autumn

The leaves fall down when the wind whistles.
The conkers fall to the ground,
They're red and round.
The fog is so thick,
It sails round and turns into a ghost
Which haunts my back garden.

Sam Ackerley (9)
Woodmansey CE Primary School, Beverley